To Everything There Is A Season

It's your season, go and live . . .

TASHEKA L. GREEN

Copyright © 2014 Tasheka L. Green All rights reserved.

All rights reserved. Except as permitted under U.S. Copyright Act of 1976, no part of this publication may be reproduced, distributed, or transmitted in any form or by any means, or stored in a database or retrieval system, without the prior written permission of the publisher.

Published by Tasheka L. Green 4/5/2014

To Everything There Is A Season
P.O. Box 342
Churchton, MD 20733
www.2eseasons.com
Phone: 1-866-478-3175

Library of Congress Cataloging in Publication Data Green, Tasheka L., 3/5/2014.

ISBN-10: 1497515157
ISBN-13: 978-1497515154

Scripture quotations are from the Holy Bible, King James Version, (KJV).

Front and back cover design by Gbenga Oyedele of Femdel, LLC www.femdel.com.

Photograph by Michael Nquantabisa of Golden Stool Photography www.goldenstoolphotos.com.

DEDICATION

In memory of my mother Deborah Christine Offer Bulgin

This book is dedicated in memory of my mother Deborah Christine Offer Bulgin. Thank you for teaching me the pillars of a virtuous woman. One who follows after God's heart and serves him with gladness. One who loves her family, and in every aspect of her life, exemplifies a woman of great strength full of purpose.

CONTENTS

	Acknowledgments	i
	Introduction	ii
	Foreword	iv
1	A Season of Change	1
2	Autumn	8
3	Winter	19
4	Spring	32
5	Summer	37
6	A New Season	42
	About the Author	52
	Deborah C. Bulgin Memorial Scholarship Foundation	55
	References	57

ACKNOWLEDGMENTS

To begin, I want to thank God, for trusting me with this work. It is in Him, I live, move, and have my being. Without God I would be nothing. Thank you Lord for all you have done for me. I worship and adore your Holy name.

Thank you to my family and friends who prayed for me, encouraged me, and supported everything that I put my hands to do. God bless you.

Thank you to Bishop Donald Wright, Dr. Nakia Wright, and the Jabbok International Fellowship Family. Bishop, you taught me the true meaning of praise, worship, and having a relationship with God. Thank you for covering me in prayer. Thank you for your wisdom and for the words of life you impart in me each week. God bless you.

Thank you to Femdel, LLC and G.K.A.M Records (God's Kingdom and Me) for believing in my vision and contributing your time and talent to this great work. God bless you.

Thank you to my children. I am so blessed to be called your mother. Mommy loves you.

Finally, to my husband, who has always taken the time to listen to my ideas, participate in my dreams, and to celebrate my accomplishments. I am blessed to have you in my life as my husband and my friend. Without your support, this book could not have been completed. I love you.

INTRODUCTION

You may ask, how can things one day be perfect and normal and in a matter of time, everything can change? Not knowing why things happen in life the way they do, one thing I do know is that God's will is good, acceptable, and it is perfect. God has led and ordered your steps in the direction that he has destined. God has been with you through this journey, never leaving or forsaking you. The process is painful, but the reward is so great. You have to go through the process in order to get to what God has prepared for you. In doing so, have faith, believe, and know, that to everything there is a season, and it is your season to live.

To Everything There Is A Season was written as part of my healing process during the death of my mother. During this time, I was at a point in my life in which I did not know what was going on. I thought my hopes were gone, my dreams had died, and my vision had faded away. In the midst of all my distress, God spoke to me and said write. I began to write, and while I was writing, God began to speak to me. The words and scriptures God gave to me healed me and brought so much peace, love, and joy. In this book, I recapture events that transpired in my life over a period of four seasons. During every season, God was right there with me. While reading this book, my prayer is that you will find the healing, peace, love, and joy you need; so that you can embrace all of the great things God has for you in this season.

FOREWORD

Many of God's children have no idea what God is saying or doing in their personal lives, in the body of Christ, or in the world precisely because they lack revelation. God said that in the last days (seasons) knowledge would increase (Daniel 12:3-4, King James Version) because it is His will to fill the earth with His glory (Numbers 14:21, King James Version). I believe that we are living in those last days, seasons in which the manifestation of His glory will be evident everywhere.

Tasheka's personal narrative is a testimony of the trials and tribulations that come with life. I believe there is a pattern here, perhaps a misunderstood principle to be relearned. Pain and struggles are often the catalysts for change—change from an old season to a new season. Seasons help us to discover who we are in Christ, as well as, the strong covenant and bond that we have with the Father, a God full of compassion and love for His children. These pages are challenging us to activate our faith to believe for miracles that appear impossible (Matthew 19:26, King James Version). This book is intended to bring us to a season that will bolster our faith. Please read it and be blessed!

Dr. Gloria A. Turner
Author & Professor

CHAPTER ONE
A SEASON OF CHANGE

The safest place in the whole wide world is in the will of God; though trials, heartaches, burdens and depression come to wear you down, you hold on to your faith and know that God is in control of your life. Who can save me, who can heal me, who can rescue me from where I am? God can heal, God can deliver, and God can break me free from all of my pain, hurt, and misery. Is this change, a season, a test, what is this? "Though he slay me, yet will I trust in him: but I will maintain mine own ways before him" (Job 13:15, King James Version). As I seek for the answers, I must endure to see the reward. "The race is not given to the swift or the battle to the strong, but to the one that endure until the end" (Ecclesiastes 9:11, King James Version). I know that God is so close to me, but yet some days he seems so far away. Lord, I need you more than I have ever needed you before. God help me, heal me, and rescue me from me; from my way of thinking and the bondage that I have placed myself in. "Many are the afflictions of the righteous: but the Lord delivereth him out of them all" (Psalms 34:19, King James Version). Only you can, only you can. There is nobody greater than you. I cry out to you, "Oh God, please turn your ear towards my voice." I need you now. "In my distress I called upon the Lord, and cried unto my God: he heard my voice out of his temple, and my cry came before him, even into his ears" (Psalms 18:6, King James Version). "And said, I cried by reason of mine affliction unto the Lord, and he heard me;

out of the belly of hell cried I, and thou heardest my voice" (Jonah 2:2, King James Version).

It all began not too long ago. Life was going as normal, but God decided to interrupt my daily plans. I remember so clearly when God whispered to me that my mother's body was stricken with cancer. No one knew, not even my mother, but God told me. What was I to do, or to say? Why did he trust me with this? They were words that I didn't want to hear, but it was God's way in preparing me and showing me what she was going and about to go through. I battled with what God had told me and did not share it with anyone, not even my mother. Was it my fault? Am I to blame? What was I to do with the message that God gave me? As time passed, my mother developed symptoms that were suppressed by ignorance and medicine. The doctors were only dealing with the symptoms and not evaluating the cause. Never getting to the core of the problem, things began to get worse and worse as time went on. She went from being severely anemic to having rheumatoid arthritis; never acknowledging the true problem. A bleeding ulcer told it all. This bleeding ulcer manifested itself with the symptoms of chronic vomiting, weight loss and severe nausea. I remember telling my mother to visit a doctor and she said she would as soon as she could get an appointment. I told her not to put it off and to go to the doctors soon. Again, she said she would do just that. After a phone call, one night with my mother, I remember dropping the phone and weeping to my husband. I wept and painfully said, "My mother is sick; she is sicker than she even knows." Why didn't I tell her? Why didn't I adhere to the voice of the Lord?

No one will ever know the pain she endured or

thoughts that were in her head. The nights she cried and prayed to the Lord. The fear that overcame her, the anxiety that shook her and the heartache that crushed her; no one will ever know.

I remember the call as if it was yesterday. My mother had only confirmed what God had already told me. My mother called and in a still calm voice she shared with me that she had stomach cancer. We had never ended a telephone conversation so quickly. Silence filled the air of my living room, and then a stream of tears flowed out of my eyes and down my pale face. Why? Why didn't I do something? The Lord had revealed it to me, and I did nothing. At that moment, I didn't share it with her, I didn't pray, I didn't ask for healing, I did nothing. Why didn't I take heed to the voice of the Lord? It was not comfortable nor was it what I wanted to hear. Why is it so important to know God's voice and to take heed? Knowing God's voice is so important and critical in our life. We need to know God's voice so that we are making the right choices for our life and so that we are able to help someone else's with their life.

God called Samuel each night and he did not answer. Instead, he answered Eli and responded, "Here I am." Eli made it known to Samuel that he did not call him. On the third encounter when Samuel ran to Eli, it was than Eli informed Samuel that it was the Lord calling him. Therefore, Eli instructed and taught Samuel to know and respond to the Lord's voice by saying, "Speak Lord for thou servant heareth" (1 Samuel 3: 9, King James Version). This time when the Lord spoke, Samuel responded and turned his ear and heart to the Lord. The Lord trusted Samuel with a word about what was going to transpire in Israel, as well as the plans that were going to be carried out against Eli. Samuel was fearful and did not want to tell Eli what the Lord had told him. However, Eli asked Samuel to tell him what the Lord had said and not to hold any words from him. Samuel proceeded to share with Eli the vision from the Lord. God used Samuel to save Eli's life. Eli was Samuel's teacher and taught him how to acknowledge and take heed to the voice of God. For Eli told Samuel if you do not tell me, something severe will happen to you.

When God gives you a word for yourself or someone else's life, take heed and do what saith the Lord. Fear not the voice of the Lord when He is speaking to you or has given you a word that irritates your ear rather than soothes it. Pay attention to the sound; the sound of His voice and the sound in your ear. For it is God speaking to you and through you. Walk out this season knowing God is with you. Follow His voice follow His will.

CHAPTER TWO
AUTUMN

"Honey I'm home and I have something to tell you." "What dear?" "I am pregnant!" What great news, every husband and wife loves to hear! Because of our love and our intimacy for one another, we have shaped and molded a child in the image of God. "So God created man in his own image, in the image of God created he him; male and female created he them" (Genesis 1:27, King James Version).

October 5, 2009, was the day that my husband and I

discovered that I was four weeks pregnant. I was excited and full of anxiousness; the first person we called was my mother. "Mom, I have something to tell you." "What is it?" she exclaimed. "We are going to have a baby!" My mother said, "Are you sure?" "Yes!" It was such a joyous time. We were all electrified about the birth of this baby. It was such a cheerful time; my husband and I had attempted for a year to conceive, but nothing happened. I began to blame myself all year for not being able to conceive. I had thought my past had scarred me for the rest of my life. But, God reminded me that I was forgiven, and he had covered and washed my past in his blood. "For he hath made him to be sin for us, who knew no sin; that we might be made the righteousness of God in him" (2 Corinthians 5:21, King James Version). Therefore, I lifted my head, encouraged myself and knew God would give me the desires of my heart. I remained prayerful and faithful to God. "Delight thyself also in the LORD and he shall give thee the desires of thine heart" (Psalms 37:4, King James Version).

And so it fell on a day. Don't know what day, but the Lord blessed my womb. There were many obstacles that I faced throughout the pregnancy. But, God covered me through them all. I was considered "high risk" because I had been diagnosed with hypertension. Therefore, for the next forty weeks, the baby and I would be closely monitored. I would have to visit both a fetal and maternal medicine physician along with my regular obstetrician. After visiting the doctor at the first appointment, she informed me that my progesterone levels were low. In order to maintain a viable pregnancy, I would have to take hormones for the first twelve weeks. Following her wisdom and praying to God, I took the hormones for the first twelve weeks of the pregnancy.

Every morning, I would always anoint my head, my husband's head and my son's head prior to leaving home. "Thou preparest a table before me in the presence of mine enemies: thou anointest my head with oil; my cup runneth over" (Psalms 23:5, King James Version). But this one particular morning, shortly after my first doctor's appointment, God instructed me to anoint my head, my heart and my stomach. I did this every morning, prior to anointing my husband's head and my son's. I did not know why God told me to do this, but I followed God's voice and instructions every day.

One would believe that having a baby would be a time full of love, joy, and happiness for a husband and a wife. However, it was not always that way. With all of the hormonal changes, I was going through, some days were not as happy as others. My husband and I had to handle everything that was taking place and still continue to let our love show for one another. We had to understand where we both were in our lives. We had to understand each other's needs as well as each other's pain. Here was the true test of intimacy. We had to see into each other's heart and help each other through the changes we were going through. Additionally, we had to help each other with what was about to take place in our lives; we had to help meet each other's needs. "And the Lord God said, it is not good that the man should be alone; I will make him a help meet for him" (Genesis 2:18, King James Version).

When I was about fifteen weeks pregnant, the doctor ordered blood work. This blood work would determine if my child were at risk for Down's syndrome. At thirty-three years old, I did not think this test was warranted, but I did continue as the doctor had ordered. When the test results returned, I was contacted by a

Genetics Counselor. She briefly explained to me the results over the phone. The blood work had indicated that my levels were above the normal range, and my child may have Down's syndrome. She invited my husband and me to discuss the results. We also had to determine if whether or not we needed to perform an amniocentesis. In doing so, this would determine with certainty if Down's syndrome were present. I hung up the phone and began to cry. I could not believe what I heard. I would have never thought that this could happen. I immediately called my husband; as soon as he answered, I just began to cry. I reiterated to him what I had discussed with the Genetics Counselor. His voice began to fade while we were talking, but I could still hear him encouraging me and telling me that everything was all right.

My husband and I went to meet with the Genetics Counselor. She began to discuss the results, go through a series of questions and explain the procedure for an amniocentesis. According to "Examed" (n.d.), "This procedure is used to collect amniotic fluid, the liquid that is in the womb. It's performed in the doctor's office. A needle is inserted through the mother's abdominal wall into the uterus, using ultrasound to guide the needle. Approximately one ounce of fluid is taken for testing. This fluid contains fetal cells that can be examined for chromosome tests. It takes about two weeks to determine if the fetus has Down's syndrome or not" (Amniocentesis). However, there were some side effects with this test, including a slight risk of miscarrying. My husband and I had a decision to make. I remember adamantly telling my husband as well as the Genetics Counselor, "I trust God, and I believe that my baby does not have Down's syndrome." I also believed that God would not allow anything to harm me or the baby. At that point, I decided to proceed with the amniocentesis. I wanted to confirm what I had already known. I scheduled an appointment for late December. My husband, who has always been fearful of needles, informed me that he would be there for me, but when they were ready to perform the procedure, he would have to step out of the room. I knew at that time, I had to call some back up. The first person I called was my mother. I asked her if she could go with me to get the procedure done. She responded, "Of course I will."

The day arrived to have the procedure performed. The nurse called us into the room. Prior to the amniocentesis, the technician showed us images of the baby through a sonogram. My husband, mother and I all had smiles that stretched across our face when we saw the baby on the screen. My mother asked with a glow, "Is that my grandchild?" We all responded, "Yes!" The doctor emphasized what he was going to do. Once he had finished speaking, my husband quietly slipped out of the room, and the needle was removed from the table. The doctor inserted the needle into my stomach. At the prick of the needle, I closed my eyes, reached out to my mother and whispered, "Mommy, hold my hand," and she did just that. The entire procedure was over in ten minutes, and now we would have to wait two weeks for the results. While I was waiting for the results, I remained prayerful and positive, believing that all was well.

As we prepared for the Christmas season, my family decided that we would have Christmas dinner at my home. My husband and I prepared our home for our family and guests. Everyone came to show their love toward one another, with food, gifts, and fun. We had such a great time laughing, playing games, and watching basketball. My mother arrived dressed in a black velour blouse and skirt adorned in sparkling gold with diamond jewelry; looking ravishing like always. She had such a great time; eating, laughing and sipping on sparkling apple cider. Being three and a half months pregnant, she assisted me by serving and cleaning. I could always count on my mother; she was always there for me. My family and I had a blissful time and decided to have another day of food and fun at my grandparent's home on New Year's Day.

On New Year's Eve, while I was preparing for church, my cellular phone rang, and it was the Genetics Counselor. She called to inform me that the test results were in. I was so anxious to hear what she had to say. She said that the test results were negative for Down's syndrome. In addition, she said, "Would you like to know the gender of the baby?" I said, "Yes, I would." She said, "You and your husband are going to have a girl." I thanked her, blessed her, and hung up the phone. I took the next moment to thank God for his word and thank God for our daughter. "Blessed art thou among women, and blessed is the fruit of thy womb" (Luke 1:42, King James Version). Immediately, I phoned my husband and mother to share with them the wonderful news. My husband said, "I told you!" And my mother laughed with joy. I went to church and blessed God with all of my power and might. "And Mary said, my soul doth magnify the Lord" (Luke 1:46, King James Version).

CHAPTER THREE
WINTER

"Happy New Year!" rang through my grandparent's home as we all began to arrive on New Year's Day for dinner. When my husband, son and I entered the house, the smell of macaroni cheese, fried chicken, collard greens, cornbread and peach cobbler appeased our appetites. We greeted one another with a hug and a smile. The children were playing outside, and the adults were battling one another in a game of dominoes. It was such a magnificent day. I noticed my mother not eating and standing afar off. Disgust and pain covered her face. I asked her what was bothering her. She began to share that she was very nauseated and did not have an appetite. She was uncertain what had triggered her sour stomach. While the family had a merry time in one part of the house, my mother stretched across the couch in the recreational room, trying to find some relief. Nothing seemed to help her. She decided to travel back home in hopes that she would get better soon. Days went by, and nothing seemed to relieve her queasiness and vomiting. Her sickness lasted for almost an entire month prior to visiting a gastroenterologist.

The Blizzard of 2010 pounded across the east coast in early February dumping three to four feet of snow in different areas throughout the state. We were trapped in our homes for almost five days and out of school and work for nearly a week and a half. Some homes were prepared for the storm, and others shared some of the distresses that they had faced during this time.

The day before the storm, my mother came to visit me at my job. During this time, we conversed over a cup of tea. I blessed her so that she could have a few things while she was at home during the storm. She called me later that night and explained how God had taken her little and made it into plenty. "I have been young, and now am old; yet have I not seen the righteous forsaken, nor his seed begging bread" (Psalms 37:25, King James Version). Although she was still feeling ill, it never stopped her from doing what she needed to do for herself and her family.

Throughout the week, my mother and I would call one another to check on each other. We both shared how this was a great time to rest, relax and enjoy our families. At this time, my mother had mentioned that she had made an appointment with a gastroenterologist to see exactly what was going on. Her appointment was scheduled for mid-February.

Once the storm had passed, I witnessed neighbors helping and digging one another out of the snow. Once driveways were shoveled, roads were clear, and the State of Emergency was lifted, business was back to normal. People returned to work, children returned to school, and the memories of the Blizzard of 2010 remained in the thoughts of everyone.

"Happy Valentine's Day!" exclaimed everyone, while we dined over steak, shrimp, and lobster. My entire family went to dinner for Valentine's Day. Fourteen of us gathered around the rectangular table and shared what we had received for Valentine's Day. I sat directly across from my mother. I could see the heaviness in her heart, and anxiety all over her face. Her appointment was the next day, and she sat in anticipation of the results. While we all indulged in steak, shrimp, and lobster; my mother grazed over a baked potato and garden salad. It bothered me to see her this way because all I wanted was for everything to be all right. My husband tuned into my feelings and attempted to make me feel better. However, his attempt failed and ended in my disgust and his fury. At this point things began to go haywire. Attitudes flared, and people began to leave the table one by one. Valentine's dinner turned into a Valentine's disaster. I reclined in my chair holding back my tears. The pain that I was feeling could not be explained. Furthermore, I did not want to add anything else to my mother's burdens and worries. That was our last dinner as an entire family. This season of love was not captured. It ended with emptiness and the thought if I could only have that moment again. "Charity suffereth long and is kind; charity envieth not; charity vaunteth, not itself, is not puffed up; Doth not behave itself unseemly, seeketh not her own, is not easily provoked, thinketh no evil; Rejoiceth not in iniquity, but rejoiceth in the truth; Beareth all things, believeth all things, hopeth all things, endureth all things. Charity never faileth: but whether there be prophecies, they shall fail; whether there be tongues, they shall cease; whether there be knowledge, it shall vanish away" (1 Corinthians 13: 4-8, King James Version).

The next day, my grandmother and aunt traveled with my mother to her doctor's appointment. The physicians informed my mother that she had a cancerous bleeding ulcer. They needed to do further testing to determine if the cancer was centralized in one location or if it had metastasized to other parts of her body. A few days had passed before the results from the Computerized Axial Tomography (CAT) Scan were discussed; the results had indicated that the cancer was localized. However, within a few weeks things had taken a drastic change and the physicians had found something differently.

My mother lost almost thirty pounds in one month, due to uncontrollable vomiting. The doctors knew they had to do something quickly. She was losing weight, nutrition and her strength. On one particular evening, soon afterward receiving the results, my mother began to vomit blood. She went to the emergency room for evaluation, and the doctor had informed her that they would need to operate the next morning. They would attempt to operate to remove the cancer or build a bypass so that she could keep food down. The next morning arrived; prayers and family members had surrounded my mother before she entered the operating room. My mother was so optimistic and showed great courage. They rolled her into the operating room, and the family walked to the waiting room. After several hours of waiting, the doctor finally came out to share with us the procedure and the results. He explained that he could not remove the cancer because it had metastasized to the liver. Therefore, he built a bypass so that she could eat and keep food on her stomach. He furthered explained that because the cancer was in a major organ and it began to metastasized that this stage was considered stage four cancer. He informed us to have my mother speak with the oncologist to discuss chemotherapy. However, before she could begin chemotherapy, she would need to heal from the surgery to regain her strength.

After the surgery, we went to see my mother in her hospital room. She tried to talk, but we wanted her to rest. I sat on the sofa and dropped my head. I had never seen my mother like this before. I was thirty-three years old, and I had never seen my mother sick, let alone in the hospital with tubes running through her nose. Again, we prayed with and for my mother, and then my family and I went home. I cried all the way home. The ride never felt so long.

Weeks had passed, and my mother remained in the hospital. She began to drink liquids and then they attempted to give her solids. Even though she was eating solids, after a few bites, she was full and did not desire the taste anymore. My mother's healing process was not going quickly. She remained in the hospital for days. She was not regaining her strength. However, she never gave up, she stayed in the race.

One day after I had visited the doctor for a routine prenatal visit, I took my mother a few 3-Dimensional Sonogram pictures of the baby. I showed my mother the pictures and informed her that her granddaughter would have her name. A light and peace came over my mother's face. We began to talk about the baby that was coming in three months.

After a month, the doctors discharged my mother from the hospital. She resided with my grandparents and remained under their care. My aunt and cousin assisted as well. They took great care of her; administering medicine, preparing meals, combing her hair and taking care of her needs. Friends and family visited my mother with cards, flowers, prayers, and encouragement.

Within weeks, I could see my mother aging and her health failing. During this time, I prayed, I fasted, I sowed, I believed and I trusted God. However, in the same manner, I worried about my mother. While I was worrying about my mother, my mother was greatly concerned about me. Even at my mother's weakest moment, she would ask me how I was feeling and how was the baby. She continually asked, "When is the baby shower?" I told her, "April 24." She told me to write it on her calendar because she wanted to make sure she was there. My mother did not want me to worry about her; she sparingly told me the information to protect me as well as the baby.

Throughout this time, my husband showed me great love and concern. Even though he had just gone through the same situation the year prior with his mother, he never left my side. My husband was still grieving, but he showed a great deal of compassion toward me. He was pouring so much love into me, but it was hard for me to pour the love back into him. I was hurting, I had questions, and I did not understand where I was and why this was happening. Our marital struggle began here. We were both empty and needed something that each other could not give at the time. We continued to go on each day, trying to find the answers and searching for a solution to our problems.

Within a week, my mother had returned to the hospital. She was retaining so much fluid that it began to build up around her lungs. When I walked into the emergency room to visit her, with her bright gray eyes, she gazed at everyone who entered. When I looked into her eyes, I knew in my heart that my mother was not going to be with me much longer.

I went to visit my mother while she was in the hospital. On that Saturday, my mother had requested that we call everyone she knew and tell them to come and see her; she wanted to tell everyone how much she loved them. As people entered the room, my mother called them by name, and one by one, she expressed her love towards them. At one point, my mother had asked everyone to leave the room because she wanted to be with her daughter. She looked up at me with her glowing hazel eyes and said, "You know that I love you and will always love you." Then she asked, "Did I do a good job in raising you?" I responded, "I love you too and you did a great job in raising me." She held my hand and wept, "Why didn't you tell me?" At that point, I couldn't answer her, I just began to cry. The conversation continued, and she asked me, "Why do I have to be first?" I began to share with my mother, how precious she was to God and how much He loved her. I whispered to her, "God wants you all to himself." We smiled, cried and expressed our love for one another.

My mother entered the hospital on Friday evening and transitioned to be with the Lord on that following Tuesday.

CHAPTER FOUR
SPRING

Birds chirping in the morning, flowers blooming everywhere, spring has begun, spring is in the air. The next few weeks were very challenging. Every day was different. Some days I smiled, some days I cried. Some days I wanted to be loved, some days I did not. Some days I talked, and other days I was speechless. My husband understood my pain, but again we both were empty and needed a void filled in our life.

During this time, I never wanted to be alone. When I was not with my husband, I was at my grandparent's home or visiting family and friends. I needed to be around family and friends. This lasted for almost four months. I just couldn't stand the thought of being alone and left with the thoughts and questions that were lingering in my head.

My family and I continued with the plans for a baby shower. The invitations were mailed, desserts were ordered, decorations were in place, and the menu was set. The day arrived for the shower. When I walked up to the venue, the first thing I noticed was the water fountain springing up from the lake. I instantly looked towards the lake and beamed. I had smiled because this was the first time the water fountain had worked after being broken for an entire year. When my mother was living, she was adamant about being at the baby shower. Remember, she had me write it on her calendar. My mother said she wanted to be there, and she was. She was not there physically, but she was there in spirit.

The guests arrived; music and laughter filled the air. My husband and I received so many wonderful gifts for the baby. We received so many items that we did not have to purchase anything. Our family and friends had truly blessed us and showed us how much they cared. It was such a beautiful day to be showered with love and gifts.

During this time, my husband and I fought to keep our marriage viable. Some day's quietness encircled our home and coldness slept in our bed. In the midst of the silence, there was tension and stress. We both wanted the peace that surpasses all understanding. "And the peace of God, which passeth all understanding, shall keep your hearts and minds through Christ Jesus" (Philippians 4:7, King James Version). Our hearts were troubled, and our minds were inattentive towards one another. No one would have ever known. We looked and acted one way in public but another way at home. We both prayed day and night that God would mend our minds, hearts and draw us closer once again. I needed my husband just as much as he needed me. We were each other's strength, he vowed to love me, and I vowed to submit. My husband and I were going to weather any storm, especially this one. "Submitting yourselves one to another in the fear of God. Wives, submit yourselves unto your own husbands, as unto the Lord. For the husband is the head of the wife, even as Christ is the head of the church: and he is the saviour of the body. Therefore as the church is subject unto Christ, so let the wives be to their own husbands in everything. Husbands, love your wives, even as Christ also loved the church, and gave himself for it; That he might sanctify and cleanse it with the washing of water by the word, that he might present it to himself a glorious church, not having spot, or wrinkle, or any such thing; but that it should be holy and without blemish" (Ephesians 5: 21-27, King James Version).

CHAPTER FIVE
SUMMER

Couple weeks before I delivered, I had a dream that I had given birth to my daughter. After giving birth, I was able to go home, but she had to remain in the hospital. In the dream, I called the hospital and asked the nurse to tell me the status of my daughter. The nurse said she could not come home; my daughter would be there for a few days. I jumped up and awoke from my sleep, left with the dream vividly in my psyche. I began to pray for my daughter and rebuke the hand of the enemy. "And this is the confidence that we have in him, that, if we ask any thing according to his will, he heareth us: And if we know that he hears us, whatsoever we ask, we know that we have the petitions that we desired of him" (1 John 5:14-15, King James Version).

Due to my pregnancy being considered "high risk," the obstetrician would not allow me to go over forty weeks. When I went to my thirty-eight weeks doctor appointment, the doctor informed me that I would be induced on June 3 at thirty-nine weeks and four days. My husband was elated, and I was fearful. As we prepared for delivery, my husband and I stayed on our face before God asking Him to bless us during labor, delivery and post-delivery. The Lord had already kept me covered by his blood and love during my pregnancy. Therefore, I knew that he was going to keep me during labor and delivery, as well. For I knew, that there is nothing too hard for God. "Alas, Lord God! Behold, you have made the heavens and the earth by your great power and by your outstretched arm! There is nothing too hard or too wonderful for you. Behold, I am the Lord, the God of all flesh; is there anything too hard for me" (Jeremiah 32:17, 27, King James Version).

Wednesday, June 2, 2010, my husband and I could hardly sleep. We were so ecstatic in knowing, that on June 3, we were going to get to see our baby girl. We both were ready to go 4:30 A.M. on Thursday, June 3, 2010. We arrived at the hospital at 5:30 A.M.; they registered me at the front desk and two nurses escorted me to my room. As soon as I entered the room, I anointed the room and every item or instrument in it. Then I proceeded to change my garments and waited for the nurse to come and complete the induction. The nurse entered the room. She started an intravenous (IV) drip, drew some blood, checked my vitals, and connected me to several machines to monitor me as well as the baby. From that point on, the contractions came slowly. At 9:00 A.M., the obstetrician came and broke my water. We briefly talked, and then she left to see her patients for the day at her office. Prior to her leaving, she stated that she would be back around 4:30 P.M. and that when she comes back, we are going to have a baby. And sure enough, when she returned, we had a beautiful baby girl, Mikayla Gabrielle Deborah Ann. When the baby was born, the doctor had determined that she had jaundice and could not depart from the hospital with me. However, I knew that she was well, and she would be able to come home soon. Again, I trusted God, and was obedient to his voice when he told me nine months prior, to anoint my head, heart, and stomach each day. The work had already been done, I just needed to walk out of the process and see his manifested power. Two days later, the nurse from the Neonatal Intensive Care Unit (NICU) called me and said, "When you come to the hospital today, you can take your baby home." I smiled, thanked God, and rejoiced.

CHAPTER SIX
A NEW SEASON

Here I am three years later still standing and remaining faithful. I have gone through so many seasons of changes. The best part about it all is that God has been with me through every season. The seasons have brought forth fruit, life, joy, happiness, and peace. It has brought me to a place in God in which I know with men things are impossible, but with God all things are possible. "But Jesus beheld *them*, and said unto them, with men this is impossible; but with God all things are possible" (Matthew 19:26, King James Version).

I still continue to ask God, "Why do you trust me with so much and with other people's situations?" His voice resonated in my ear, "Many are called, but a few are chosen." "And you were chosen to do this even before you entered into your mother's womb" (Matthew 22:14, King James Version). "Before I formed thee in the belly I knew thee; and before thou camest forth out of the womb I sanctified thee, and I ordained thee a prophet unto the nations" (Jeremiah 1:5, King James Version).

Are you still asking how can things one day go perfect and normal and in a matter of time, everything can change? The answer is, your life is not yours, you belong to God. "For I know the plans I have for you," declares the LORD, "plans to prosper you and not to harm you, plans to give you hope and a future. Then you will call on me and come and pray to me, and I will listen to you. You will seek me and find me when you seek me with all your heart"

(Jeremiah 29:11-13, King James Version). God's will is good, acceptable, and it is perfect. "And be not conformed to this world: but be ye transformed by the renewing of your mind, that ye may prove what is that good, and acceptable, and perfect, will of God" (Romans 12:2, King James Version). He will never lead your steps in the direction in which he did not order. God has been with you during your seasons. "The steps of a good man are ordered by the LORD: and he delighteth in his way" (Psalms 37:23, King James Version). In life, you will encounter many events. Regardless of what life brings, you must understand that to everything there is a season, and a time to every purpose under the heaven. You must press toward the mark each day and run after all that God has for you. "I press toward the mark for the prize of the high calling of God in Christ Jesus" (Philippians 3:14, King James

Version).

"To everything there is a season, and a time to every purpose under the heaven: A time to be born, and a time to die; a time to plant, and a time to pluck up that which is planted; A time to kill, and a time to heal; a time to break down, and a time to build up; A time to weep, and a time to laugh; a time to mourn, and a time to dance; A time to cast away stones, and a time to gather stones together; a time to embrace, and a time to refrain from embracing; A time to get, and a time to lose; a time to keep, and a time to cast away; A time to rend, and a time to sew; a time to keep silence, and a time to speak; A time to love, and a time to hate; a time of war, and a time of peace. What profit hath he that worketh in that wherein he laboureth? I have seen the travail, which God hath given to the sons of men to be exercised in it. He hath made everything beautiful in his time: also he hath set the world in their heart, so that no man can find out the work that God maketh from the beginning to the end. I know that there is no good in them, but for a man to rejoice, and to do good

in his life. And also that every man should eat and drink, and enjoy the good of all his labour, it is the gift of God. I know that, whatsoever God doeth, it shall be forever: nothing can be put to it, nor any thing taken from it: and God doeth it, that men should fear before him. That which hath been is now; and that which is to be hath already been; and God requireth that which is past" (Ecclesiastes 3: 1-15, King James Version).

Merriam Webster dictionary defined season as a time characterized by a particular circumstance or feature. Trust the process or the season you are in. God ordained this particular time for your life. Hold on to what you believe, God will take care of you. God will never leave you or forsake you. "Keep your lives free from the love of money and be content with what you have because God has said, never will I leave you; never will I forsake you" (Hebrews 13:5, King James Version). Stand still and know that this season will pass, and blessed be the God who changes the season. "And he changeth the times and the seasons: he removeth kings, and setteth up kings: he giveth wisdom unto the wise and knowledge to them that know understanding" (Daniel 2:21, King James Version). Your new season begins today when you speak and call forth a new season. Regardless of where you are in the process, you are in the will of God, for you are His will. Yeah and Amen! "For all the promises of God in him are yea, and in him Amen, unto the glory of God by us" (2 Corinthians 1:20, King James Version).

You must go where God leads, you must glow so people can see, you must grow where you are and live with what God left you. So many times in our life, we sit and wonder why. God has us where he does, a living sacrifice, to be an example to the world; so that everyone can see, all His goodness, and His mercy, how His grace covers us. He has done so many things that we can't complain. All we do is continue to know that He will make away. You must go where God leads, you must glow so people can see, you must grow where you are and live with what God left you. Many are the plans of man, but only God's plan will prevail, (Proverbs 19:21, King James Version). Don't be weary in well doing; all you have to do is keep going. Have faith and believe, and know one day you will receive, all the blessings that are for you, He is going to see you through. "And let us not be weary in well doing: for in due season, we shall reap if we faint not" (Galatians 6:9, King James Version). Your steps are ordered, and guided by the Lord. "The steps of a good man are ordered by the LORD: and he delighteth in his way" (Psalms 37:23, King James Version). They lead to His promises and all open doors. You must go where God leads, you must glow so people can see, you must grow where you are and live with what God left you. Greater is He that's in you, than He that's in the world. You are an overcomer; you're more than a conqueror. "Ye are of God, little children, and have overcome them: because greater is he that is in you than he that is in the world" (1 John 4:4, King James Version). He left his love. He left his joy. He left his peace, and you must go and live with what God has left you.

To everything there is a season, to everything there is a time, to everything there is a purpose, and God will reveal it to you in time. Wait on the Lord, and be of good courage, wait on the Lord, and be strong, wait on the Lord, and be faithful, God will reveal it to you in time. "Wait on the LORD: be of good courage, and he shall strengthen thine heart: wait, I say, on the LORD" (Psalms 27:14, King James Version). For eyes haven't seen nor ears have heard, neither have it entered into the heart of man. The great things God has in stored for you. The great things God has prepared for you. "But as it is written, eye hath not seen, nor ear heard, neither have entered into the heart of man, the things which God hath prepared for them that love him" (1 Corinthians 2:9, King James Version). God will reveal it in time. It's your season, go and live.

Say these words with me, "Whatever season I am in, it is worth it all. Now, I ask you Lord to anoint my life, anoint my light and anoint my heart. It's my season, I will go and live."

Write your vision for this season, make it plain, and run after your promise. "And the LORD answered me, and said, Write the vision, and make *it* plain upon tables, that he may run that readeth it" (Habakkuk 2:2, King James Version).

My vision for this season is...

ABOUT THE AUTHOR

From her professionalism, to her integrity, to her creative teaching, motivating, and leading skills, Tasheka Lynnise Green works hard to ensure that everyone she meets reaches their maximum potential. Her heart is after anything that will benefit people in general and their journey to greatness. She encourages everyone she meets to greatness and ensures that they get there.

Tasheka is the eldest daughter of Leon Sellman and the late Deborah Offer Bulgin. She was raised in Churchton, Maryland. Currently, Tasheka resides in Maryland with her husband William, and three children. She is the proud mother of a handsome 16 year old son, Marquis, a beautiful 3 year old daughter Mikayla, and a charming baby boy, 1 year old William Jr. She spends her weekends with her family and embraces every moment life has to offer.

Tasheka attended Anne Arundel County Public Schools. She completed her undergraduate and graduate studies from Bowie State University. She holds a Bachelor's of Science degree in Elementary Education and a Master's of Education degree in Administration and Supervision. Currently, she is pursuing a Doctorate in Educational Leadership from the University of Phoenix.

She has used her educational background to teach elementary, undergraduate, and post-graduate students. She has served in the field of education for thirteen years, providing educational guidance to teachers, students, parents, and community leaders. Tasheka's educational role ranges from a classroom teacher, gifted and talented teacher, behavior intervention specialist, and currently a principal.

Tasheka's love for God and writing led her to write a play entitled, *Don't Stop Giving God Praises, Cause Tomorrow Might Be Too Late (1994)*. Also, she wrote the gospel songs, *Go Where God Leads (2014), I Come to Worship and Bless Your Name (2014),* and *To Everything There Is A Season (2014)*. In addition, Tasheka is the author of *Words in my Pocket (2013)*, a math vocabulary game which supports children's conceptual understanding with math. She is in the process of writing a resource tool for principals to help them distinguish between being and instructional leader and administrator.

Tasheka L. Green is a leader, educator, motivational speaker, and personal life coach. Currently, she is the Principal of Pershing Hill Elementary School. She is highly respected by the students, parents and fellow colleagues.

Tasheka is the President and Founder of *To Everything There Is A Season: Deborah C. Bulgin Memorial Scholarship Foundation, Incorporation*. The foundation awards scholarships to young minority women entering into an accredited college program.

Tasheka received her early studies of the bible at Franklin United Methodist Church attending Sunday school and worship services. She received Jesus as her personal savior the first Sunday in January of 1994. Presently, Tasheka attends Jabbok International Fellowship in Forestville, Maryland under the leadership of Bishop Donald A. Wright. She has sung with several gospel groups including Essence of Praise, Unlimited Praise Mass Choir, and Positive Perspective. She has shared stages with artist such as John P. Key, Hezekiah Walker and James Hall. Tasheka has attended several bible classes, workshops, seminars and conferences to enhance her knowledge of Jesus.

Tasheka's desire is to walk in the ways of a virtuous women (Proverbs 31:1-31), to be in the center of God's will, impact change, and to be an example of Christ in the earth.

TO EVERYTHING THERE IS A SEASON: IT'S YOUR SEASON GO AND LIVE

Deborah C. Bulgin Memorial Scholarship Foundation

The *Deborah C. Bulgin Memorial Scholarship Foundation* was established in 2014 as a memorial for Deborah Christine Offer Bulgin, a studious and virtuous woman who lost her life to stage four stomach cancer in 2010. Deborah was an individual of extraordinary vision, talent, presence, and accomplishment. A born leader, Deborah worked in the church, educational endeavors, local and civic organizations with a view toward making situations better than she found them.

The second child of Lawrence and Alverta Offer, Deborah was born October 4, 1956, in Churchton, Maryland, where she attended Anne Arundel County Public Schools. Graduating with honors from Sojourner Douglass College, Deborah obtained a Bachelors of Arts and a Masters of Arts degree in Business Administration. Deborah was unfailing in advocating a strong educational background. Deborah's emphasis on education provides the basis for the establishment of this scholarship fund in her memory. It favors students, especially young minority women, interested in majoring in Business Administration.

Her life and legacy will continue to live on by awarding scholarships to deserving scholars, so that they can pursue their dreams and visions.

TO EVERYTHING THERE IS A SEASON: IT'S YOUR SEASON GO AND LIVE

Deborah C. Bulgin Memorial Scholarship

Show your support at the link below...

www.GoFundMe.com/7xgfgs

 Visit using your phone!

REFERENCES

"season." Merriam-Webster.com. 2014. http://www.merriam-webster.com (27 December 2013).

New King James Version. Bible Gateway. Web. 15 April 2010.

New King James Version. Bible Hub. Web. 15 April 2010.

ExaMed. (n.d.). Retrieved from http://www.examed.hu/enhtml.

Made in the USA
San Bernardino, CA
23 April 2014